Margarita Waters, OSB

Al Moda Sandles

Meditation

Padmasambhava: "Looks Like Me."

Padmasambhava, the "Precious Master," "Guru Rinpoche," is the founder of Tibetan Buddhism, and the Buddha of our time. It is believed that, on seeing this statue at Samye in Tibet, where it was made in the eighth century, he remarked, "It looks like me," and then blessed it, saying, "Now it is the same as me!"

Meditation

Sogyal Rinpoche

Edited by
Patrick Gaffney
and
Andrew Harvey

HarperSanFrancisco
A Division of HarperCollins*Publishers*

For information address HarperCollins Publishers, 10 East 53rd Street, New York, NY 10022.

This little book is chapter 5 of *The Tibetan Book of Living and Dying.*

This edition is printed on acid-free paper that meets the American National Standards Institute Z39.48 Standard.

Library of Congress Cataloging-in-Publication Data
Sogyal, Rinpoche.
Meditation / Sogyal Rinpoche. – 1st Harper paperback ed.
p. cm.
ISBN 0-06-251114-9
1. Meditation–Buddhism. I. Title
BQ5612.S64 1994 94-13757
294.3'443–dc20 CIP

02 03 HAD 10 9 8

Bringing the Mind Home

Over 2,500 years ago, a man who had been searching for the truth for many, many lifetimes came to a quiet place in northern India and sat down under a tree. He continued to sit under the tree, with immense resolve, and vowed not to get up until he had found the truth. At dusk, it is said, he conquered all the dark forces of delusion; and early the next morning, as the star Venus broke in the dawn sky, the man was rewarded for his age-long patience, discipline, and flawless concentration by achieving the final goal of human existence, enlightenment. At that sacred moment, the earth itself shuddered, as if "drunk with bliss," and as the scriptures tell us, "No one anywhere was angry, ill, or sad; no one did evil, none was proud; the world became quite quiet, as though it had reached full perfection." This man became known as the Buddha. Here is the Vietnamese master Thich Nhat Hanh's beautiful description of the Buddha's enlightenment:

> *Gautama felt as though a prison which had confined him for thousands of lifetimes had broken open. Ignorance had been the jailkeeper. Because of ignorance, his mind had been obscured, just like the moon and stars hidden by the storm clouds. Clouded by*

endless waves of deluded thoughts, the mind had falsely divided reality into subject and object, self and others, existence and non-existence, birth and death, and from these discriminations arose wrong views—the prisons of feelings, craving, grasping, and becoming. The suffering of birth, old age, sickness, and death only made the prison walls thicker. The only thing to do was to seize the jailkeeper and see his true face. The jailkeeper was ignorance. . . . Once the jail-keeper was gone, the jail would disappear and never be rebuilt again.[1]

What the Buddha saw was that ignorance of our true nature is the root of all the torment of samsara,[2] and the root of ignorance itself is our mind's habitual tendency to distraction. To end the mind's distraction would be to end samsara itself; the key to this, he realized, is to bring the mind home to its true nature, through the practice of meditation.

The Buddha sat in serene and humble dignity on the ground, with the sky above him and around him, as if to show us that in meditation you sit with an open, sky-like attitude of mind, yet remain present, earthed, and grounded. The sky is our absolute nature, which has no barriers and is boundless, and the ground is our reality, our relative, ordinary condition. The posture we take when we meditate signifies that we are linking absolute and relative, sky and ground, heaven and earth, like two wings of a bird, integrating the sky-like deathless nature of mind and the ground of our transient, mortal nature.

The gift of learning to meditate is the greatest gift you can give yourself in this life. For it is only through meditation that you can undertake the journey to discover your true nature, and so find the stability and confidence you will need to live, and die, well. Meditation is the road to enlightenment.

Training the Mind

There are so many ways to present meditation, and I must have taught on it a thousand times, but each time it is different, and each time it is direct and fresh.

Fortunately we live in a time when all over the world many people are becoming familiar with meditation. It is being increasingly accepted as a practice that cuts through and soars above cultural and religious barriers, and enables those who pursue it to establish a direct contact with the truth of their being. It is a practice that at once transcends the dogma of religions and is the essence of religions.

Generally we waste our lives, distracted from our true selves, in endless activity; meditation, on the other hand, is the way to bring us back to ourselves, where we can really experience and taste our full being, beyond all habitual patterns. Our lives are lived in intense and anxious struggle, in a swirl of speed and aggression, in competing, grasping, possessing, and achieving, forever burdening ourselves with extraneous activities and preoccupations. Meditation is the exact opposite. To meditate is to make a complete break with how we "normally" operate, for it is a state free of all cares and concerns, in which there is no competition, no desire to possess or grasp at anything, no intense and anxious struggle, and no hunger to achieve: an ambitionless state where there is neither acceptance nor rejection, neither hope nor fear, a state in which we slowly begin to release all those emotions and concepts that have imprisoned us into the space of natural simplicity.

The Buddhist meditation masters know how flexible and workable the mind is. If we train it, anything is possible. In fact, we are already perfectly trained by and for samsara, trained to get jealous, trained to grasp, trained to be anxious and sad and desperate and greedy, trained to react angrily to whatever provokes us. We are trained, in fact, to such an extent that these negative emotions rise spontaneously, without our even trying to generate them. So everything is a question of training and the power of habit. Devote the mind to confusion and we know only too well, if we're honest, that it will become a dark master of confusion, adept in its addictions, subtle and perversely supple in its slaveries. Devote it in meditation to the task of freeing itself from illusion, and we will find that with time, patience, discipline, and the right training, our mind will begin to unknot itself and know its essential bliss and clarity.

"Training" the mind does not in any way mean forcibly subjugating or brainwashing the mind. To train the mind is first to see directly and concretely how the mind functions, a knowledge that you derive from spiritual teachings and through personal experience in meditation practice. Then you can use that understanding to tame the mind and work with it skillfully, to make it more and more pliable, so that you can become master of your own mind and employ it to its fullest and most beneficial end.

The eighth-century Buddhist master Shantideva said:

If this elephant of mind is bound on all sides
by the cord of mindfulness,
All fear disappears and complete happiness
comes.
All enemies: all the tigers, lions, elephants,
bears, serpents [of our emotions];[3]
And all the keepers of hell; the demons and
the horrors,
All of these are bound by the mastery of your
mind,
And by the taming of that one mind, all are
subdued,
Because from the mind are derived all fears
and immeasurable sorrows.[4]

Just as a writer only learns a spontaneous freedom of expression after years of often grueling study, and just as the simple grace of a dancer is achieved only with enormous, patient effort, so when you begin to understand where meditation will lead you, you will approach it as the greatest endeavor of your life, one that demands of you the deepest perseverance, enthusiasm, intelligence, and discipline.

The Heart of Meditation

The purpose of meditation is to awaken in us the sky-like nature of mind, and to introduce us to that which we really are, our unchanging pure awareness, which underlies the whole of life and death.

In the stillness and silence of meditation, we glimpse and return to that deep inner nature that we have so long ago lost sight of amid the busyness and distraction of our minds. Isn't it extraordinary that our minds cannot stay still for longer than a few moments without grasping after distraction; they are so restless and preoccupied that sometimes I think that living in a city in the modern world, we are already like the tormented beings in the intermediate state after death, where the consciousness is said to be agonizingly restless. According to some authorities, up to 13 percent of people in the United States suffer from some kind of mental disorder. What does that say about the way we live?

We are fragmented into so many different aspects. We don't know who we really are, or what aspects of ourselves we should identify with or believe in. So many contradictory voices, dictates, and feelings fight for control over our inner lives that we find ourselves scattered everywhere, in all directions, leaving nobody at home.

Meditation, then, is bringing the mind home.

In the teaching of Buddha, we say there are three things that make all the difference between your meditation being merely a way of bringing temporary relaxation, peace, and bliss, or of becoming a powerful cause for your enlightenment and the enlightenment of others. We call them: "Good in the Beginning, Good in the Middle, and Good at the End."

Good in the Beginning springs from the awareness that we and all sentient beings fundamentally have the buddha nature as our innermost essence, and that to realize it is to be free of ignorance and to put an end, finally, to suffering. So each time we begin our practice of meditation, we are moved by this, and inspire ourselves with the motivation to dedicate our practice, and our life, to the enlightenment of all beings in the spirit of this prayer, which all the buddhas of the past have prayed:

By the power and the truth of this practice:
May all beings have happiness, and the causes of happiness;
May all be free from sorrow, and the causes of sorrow;
May all never be separated from the sacred happiness which is sorrowless;
And may all live in equanimity, without too much attachment and too much aversion,
And live believing in the equality of all that lives.

Good in the Middle is the frame of mind with which we enter into the heart of the practice, one inspired by the realization of the nature of mind, from which arises an attitude of non-grasping, free of any conceptual reference whatsoever, and an awareness that all things are inherently "empty," illusory, and dream-like.

Good at the End is the way in which we bring our meditation to a close by dedicating all its merit, and praying with real fervor: "May whatever merit that comes from this practice go toward the enlightenment of all beings; may it become a drop in the ocean of the activity of all the buddhas in their tireless work for the liberation of all beings." Merit is the positive power and benefit, the peace and happiness that radiate from your practice. You dedicate this merit for the long-term, ultimate benefit of beings, for their enlightenment. On a more immediate level, you dedicate it so that there may be peace in the world, so that everyone may be entirely free of want and illness, and experience total well-being and lasting happiness. Then, realizing the illusory and dream-like nature of reality, you reflect on how, in the deepest sense, you who are dedicating your practice, those to whom you are dedicating it, and even the very act of dedication are all inherently "empty" and illusory. This is said in the teachings to seal the meditation and ensure that none of its pure power can leak or seep away, and so ensure that none of the merit of your practice is ever wasted.

These three sacred principles—the skillful *motivation,* the *attitude of non-grasping* that secures the practice, and the *dedication* that seals it—are what make your meditation truly enlightening and powerful. They have been beautifully described by the great Tibetan master Longchenpa as "the heart, the eye, and the life-force of true practice." As Nyoshul Khenpo says: "To accomplish complete enlightenment, more than this is not necessary: but less than this is incomplete."

The Practice of Mindfulness

Meditation is bringing the mind back home, and this is first achieved through the practice of mindfulness.

Once an old woman came to Buddha and asked him how to meditate. He told her to remain aware of every movement of her hands as she drew the water from the well, knowing that if she did, she would soon find herself in that state of alert and spacious calm that is meditation.

The practice of mindfulness, of bringing the scattered mind home, and so of bringing the different aspects of our being into focus, is called "Peacefully Remaining" or "Calm Abiding." "Peacefully Remaining" accomplishes three things. First, all the fragmented aspects of ourselves, which had been at war, settle and dissolve and become friends. In that settling we begin to understand ourselves more, and sometimes even have glimpses of the radiance of our fundamental nature.

Second, the practice of mindfulness deffuses our negativity, aggression, and turbulent emotions, which may have been gathering power over many lifetimes. Rather than suppressing emotions or indulging in them, here it is important to view them, and your thoughts, and whatever arises with an acceptance and generosity that are as open and spacious as possible. Tibetan masters say that this wise generosity has the flavor of boundless space, so warm and cozy that you feel enveloped and protected by it, as if by a blanket of sunlight.

Gradually, as you remain open and mindful, and use one of the techniques that I will explain later to focus your mind more and more, your negativity will slowly be defused; you begin to feel well in your being, or as the French say, *être bien dans sa peau* (well in your own skin). From this comes release and a profound ease. I think of this practice as the most effective form of therapy and self-healing.

Third, this practice unveils and reveals your essential Good Heart, because it dissolves and removes the unkindness or the harm in you. Only when we have removed the harm in ourselves do we become truly useful to others. Through the practice, then, by slowly removing the unkindness and harm from ourselves, we allow our true Good Heart, the fundamental goodness and kindness that are our real nature, to shine out and become the warm climate in which our true being flowers.

You will see now why I call meditation the true practice of peace, the true practice of nonaggression and nonviolence, and the real and greatest disarmament.

Natural Great Peace

When I teach meditation, I often begin by saying: "Bring your mind home. And release. And relax."

The whole of meditation practice can be essentialized into these three crucial points: bring your mind home, and release, and relax. Each phrase contains meanings that resonate on many levels.

To *bring your mind home* means to bring the mind into the state of Calm Abiding through the practice of mindfulness. In its deepest sense, to bring your mind home is to turn your mind inward and to rest in the nature of mind. This itself is the highest meditation.

To *release* means to release mind from its prison of grasping, since you recognize that all pain and fear and distress arise from the craving of the grasping mind. On a deeper level, the realization and confidence that arise from your growing understanding of the nature of mind inspire the profound and natural generosity that enables you to release all grasping from your heart, letting it free itself, to melt away in the inspiration of meditation.

Finally, to *relax* means to be spacious and to relax the mind of its tensions. More deeply, you relax into the true nature of your mind, the state of Rigpa. The Tibetan words that evoke this process suggest the sense of "relaxing *upon* the Rigpa." It is like pouring a handful of sand onto a flat surface; each grain settles of its own accord. This is how you relax into your true nature, letting all thoughts and emotions naturally subside and dissolve into the state of the nature of mind.

When I meditate, I am always inspired by this poem by Nyoshul Khenpo:

Rest in natural great peace
This exhausted mind
Beaten helpless by karma and neurotic
thought,
Like the relentless fury of the pounding
waves
In the infinite ocean of samsara.

Rest in natural great peace.

Above all, be at ease, be as natural and spacious as possible. Slip quietly out of the noose of your habitual anxious self, release all grasping, and relax into your true nature. Think of your ordinary, emotional, thought-ridden self as a block of ice or a slab of butter left out in the sun. If you are feeling hard and cold, let this aggression melt away in the sunlight of your meditation. Let peace work on you and enable you to gather your scattered mind into the mindfulness of Calm Abiding, and awaken in you the awareness and insight of Clear Seeing. And you will find all your negativity disarmed, your aggression dissolved, and your confusion evaporating slowly, like mist into the vast and stainless sky of your absolute nature.[5]

Quietly sitting, body still, speech silent, mind at peace, let thoughts and emotions, whatever rises, come and go, without clinging to anything.

What does this state feel like? Dudjom Rinpoche used to say, imagine a man who comes home after a long, hard day's work in the fields, and sinks into his favorite chair in front of the fire. He has been working all day and he knows that he has achieved what he wanted to achieve; there is nothing more to worry about, nothing left unaccomplished, and he can let go completely of all his cares and concerns, content, simply, to be.

So when you meditate, it is essential to create the right inner environment of the mind. All effort and struggle come from not being spacious, and so creating that right environment is vital for your meditation truly to happen. When humor and spaciousness are present, meditation arises effortlessly.

Sometimes when I meditate, I don't use any particular method. I just allow my mind to rest, and find, especially when I am inspired, that I can bring my mind home and relax very quickly. I sit quietly and rest in the nature of mind; I don't question or doubt whether I am in the "correct" state or not. There is no effort, only rich understanding, wakefulness, and unshakable certainty. When I am in the nature of mind, the ordinary mind is no longer there. I simply am. A fundamental trust is present. There is nothing in particular to do.

Methods in Meditation

If your mind is able to settle naturally of its own accord, and if you find you are inspired simply to rest in its pure awareness, then you do not need any method of meditation. In fact, it might even be unskillful when you're in such a state to try to employ one. However, the vast majority of us find it difficult to arrive at that state straight away. We simply do not know how to awaken it, and our minds are so wild and so distracted that we need a skillful means, a method to evoke it.

By "skillful" I mean that you bring together your understanding of the essential nature of your mind, your knowledge of your own various, shifting moods, and the insight you have developed through your practice into how to work with yourself, from moment to moment. By bringing these together, you learn the art of applying whatever method is appropriate for any particular situation or problem, to transform that environment of your mind.

But remember: A method is only a means, *not* the meditation itself. It is through practicing the method skillfully that you reach the perfection of that pure state of total presence, which is the real meditation.

There is a revealing Tibetan saying, "*Gompa ma yin, kompa yin,*" which means literally: "'Meditation' is not; 'getting used to' is." It means that meditation is nothing other than getting used to the *practice* of meditation. As it is said, "Meditation is not striving, but naturally becoming assimilated into it." As you continue to practice the method, then meditation slowly arises. Meditation is not something that you can "do," it is something that has to happen spontaneously, only when we have perfected the practice.

However, for meditation to happen, calm and auspicious conditions have to be created. Before we have mastery over our mind, we need first to calm its environment. At the moment, mind is like a candle flame: unstable, flickering, constantly changing, fanned by the violent winds of our thoughts and emotions. The flame will only burn steadily when we can calm the air around it; so we can only begin to glimpse and rest in the nature of mind when we have stilled the turbulence of our thoughts and emotions. On the other hand, once we have found a stability in our meditation, noises and disturbances of every

kind will have far less impact.

In the West, people tend to be absorbed by what I would call "the technology of meditation." The modern world, after all, is fascinated by mechanisms and machines, and addicted to purely practical formulae. But by far the most important feature of meditation is not the technique, but the spirit: the skillful, inspired, and creative way in which we practice, which could also be called "the posture."

The Posture

The masters say: "If you create an auspicious condition in your body and your environment, then meditation and realization will automatically arise." Talk about posture is not esoteric pedantry; the whole point of assuming a correct posture is to create a more inspiring environment for meditation, for the awakening of Rigpa. There is a connection between the posture of the body and the attitude of the mind. Mind and body are interrelated, and meditation arises naturally once your posture and attitude are inspired.

If you are sitting, and your mind is not wholly in tune with your body—if you are, for instance, anxious and preoccupied with something—then your body will experience physical discomfort and difficulties arise more easily. Whereas if your mind is in a calm, inspired state, it will influence your whole posture, and you can sit much more naturally and effortlessly. So it is very important to unite the posture of your body and the confidence that arises from your realization of the nature of mind.

The posture I am going to explain to you may differ slightly from others you may be used to. It comes from the ancient teachings of Dzogchen and is the one my masters taught me, and I have found it extremely powerful.

In the Dzogchen teachings it is said that *your View and your posture* should be like a mountain. Your View is the summation of your whole understanding and insight into the nature of mind, which you bring to your meditation. So your View translates into and inspires your posture, expressing the core of your being in the way you sit.

Sit, then, as if you were a mountain, with all the unshakable, steadfast majesty of a mountain. A mountain is completely natural and at ease with itself, however strong the winds that try to batter it, however thick the dark clouds that swirl around its peak. Sitting like a mountain, let your mind rise and fly and soar.

The most essential point of this posture is to keep the back straight, like "an arrow" or "a pile of golden coins." The "inner energy" or *prana* will then flow easily through the subtle channels of the body, and your mind will find its true state of rest. Don't force anything. The lower part of the spine has a natural curve; it should be relaxed but upright. Your head should be balanced comfortably on your neck. It is your shoulders and the upper part of your torso that carry the strength and grace of the posture, and they should be held in strong poise, but without any tension.

Sit with your legs crossed. You do not have to sit in the full-lotus posture, which is emphasized more in advanced yoga practice. The crossed legs express the unity of life and death, good and bad, skillful means and wisdom, masculine and feminine principles, samsara and *nirvana;* the humor of non-duality.

You may also choose to sit on a chair, with your legs relaxed, but be sure always to keep your back straight.[6]

In my tradition of meditation, your eyes should be kept open: this is a very important point. If you are sensitive to disturbances from outside, when you begin to practice you may find it helpful to close your eyes for a while and quietly turn within.

Once you feel established in calm, gradually open your eyes, and you will find your gaze has grown more peaceful and tranquil. Now look downwards, along the line of your nose, at an angle of about 45 degrees in front of you. One practical tip in general is that whenever your mind is wild, it is best to lower your gaze, and whenever it is dull and sleepy, to bring the gaze up.

Once your mind is calm and the clarity of insight begins to arise, you will feel free to bring your gaze up, opening your eyes more and looking into the space directly in front of you. This is the gaze recommended in the Dzogchen practice.

In the Dzogchen teachings it is said that *your meditation and your gaze* should be like the vast expanse of a great ocean; all-pervading, open, and limitless. Just as your View and posture are inseparable, so your meditation inspires your gaze, and they now merge as one.

Do not focus on anything in particular; instead, turn back into yourself slightly, and let your gaze expand and become more and more spacious and pervasive. You will discover that your vision itself becomes more expansive, and that there is more peace, more compassion in your gaze, more equanimity, and more poise.

The Tibetan name of the Buddha of Compassion is Chenrézig, *Chen* is the eye, *ré* is the corner of the eye, and *zig* means see. This signifies that with his compassionate eyes Chenrézig sees the needs of all beings. So direct the compassion that radiates from your meditation, softly and gently, through your eyes, so that your gaze becomes the very gaze of compassion itself, all-pervasive and ocean-like.

There are several reasons for keeping the eyes open. With the eyes open, you are less likely to fall asleep. Then, meditation is not a means of running away from the world, or of escaping from it into a trance-like experience of an altered state of consciousness. On the contrary, it is a direct way to help us truly understand ourselves, and relate to life and the world.

Therefore, in meditation, you keep your eyes open, not closed. Instead of shutting out life, you remain open and at peace with everything. You leave all your senses—hearing, seeing, feeling—just open, naturally, as they are, without grasping after their perceptions. As Dudjom Rinpoche said: "Though different forms are perceived, they are in essence empty; yet in the emptiness one perceives forms. Though different sounds are heard, they are empty; yet in the emptiness one perceives sounds. Also different thoughts arise; they are empty, yet in the emptiness one perceives thoughts." Whatever you see, whatever you hear, leave it as it is, without grasping. Leave the hearing in the hearing, leave the seeing in the seeing, without letting your attachment enter into the perception.

According to the special luminosity practice of Dzogchen, all the light of our wisdom-energy resides in the heart center, which is connected through "wisdom channels" to the eyes. The eyes are the "doors" of the luminosity, so you keep them open, in order not to block these wisdom channels.[7]

When you meditate keep your mouth slightly open, as if about to say a deep, relaxing "Aaaah." By keeping the mouth slightly open and breathing mainly through the mouth, it is said that the "karmic winds" that create discursive thoughts are normally less likely to arise, and create obstacles in your mind and meditation.

Rest your hands comfortably covering your knees. This is called the "mind in comfort and ease" posture.

There is a spark of hope, a playful humor, about this posture, which lies in the secret understanding that we all have the buddha nature. So when you assume this posture, you are playfully imitating a buddha, acknowledging and giving real encouragement to the emergence of your own buddha nature. You begin in fact to respect yourself as a potential buddha. At the same time, you still recognize your relative condition. But because you have let yourself be inspired by a joyful trust in your own true buddha nature, you can accept your negative aspects more easily and deal with them more kindly and with more humor. When you meditate, then, invite yourself to feel the self-esteem, the dignity, and strong humility of the buddha that you are. I often say that if you simply let yourself be inspired by this joyful trust, it is enough: out of this understanding and confidence meditation will naturally arise.

Three Methods of Meditation

The Buddha taught 84,000 different ways to tame and pacify the negative emotions, and in Buddhism there are countless methods of meditation. I have found three meditation techniques that are particularly effective in the modern world, and which anyone can use and benefit from. They are "watching" the breath, using an object, and reciting a mantra.

1. "WATCHING" THE BREATH

The first method is very ancient and found in all schools of Buddhism. It is to rest your attention, lightly and mindfully, on the breath.

Breath *is* life, the basic and most fundamental expression of our life. In Judaism *ruah,* the breath, means the spirit of God that infuses the creation; in Christianity also there is a profound link between the Holy Spirit, without which nothing could have life, and the breath. In the teaching of Buddha, the breath, or *prana* in Sanskrit, is said to be "the vehicle of the mind," because it is the prana that makes our mind move. So when you calm the mind by working skillfully with the breath, you are simultaneously and automatically taming and training the mind. Haven't we all experienced how relaxing it can be when life becomes stressful, to be alone for a few minutes and just breathe, in and out, deeply and quietly? Even such a simple exercise can help us a great deal.

So when you meditate breathe naturally, just as you always do. Focus your awareness lightly on the outbreath. When you breathe out, just flow out with the outbreath. Each time you breathe out, you are letting go and releasing all your grasping. Imagine your breath dissolving into the all-pervading expanse of truth. Each time you breathe out, and before you breathe in again, you will find that there will be a natural gap, as the grasping dissolves.

Rest in that gap, in that open space. And when, naturally, you breathe in, don't focus especially on the inbreath but go on resting your mind in the gap that has opened up.

When you are practicing, it's important not to get involved in mental commentary, analysis, or internal gossip. Do not mistake the running commentary in your mind ("Now I'm breathing in, now I'm breathing out") for mindfulness; what is important is pure presence.

Don't concentrate too much on the breath; give it about 25 percent of your attention, with the other 75 percent quietly and spaciously relaxed. As you become more mindful of your breathing, you will find that you become more and more present, gather all your scattered aspects back into yourself, and become whole.

Rather than "watching" the breath, let yourself gradually identify with it, as if you were becoming it. Slowly the breath, the breather, and the breathing become one; duality and separation dissolve.

You will find that this very simple process of mindfulness filters your thoughts and emotions. Then, as if you were shedding an old skin, something is peeled off and freed.

Some people, however, are not relaxed or at ease with watching the breathing; they find it almost claustrophobic. For them, the next technique might be very helpful.

2. USING AN OBJECT

A second method, which many people find useful, is to rest the mind lightly on an object. You can use an object of natural beauty that invokes a special feeling of inspiration for you, such as a flower or crystal. But something that embodies the truth, such as an image of the Buddha, or Christ, or particularly your master, is even more powerful. Your master is your living link with the truth;

and because of your personal connection to your master, just seeing his or her face connects you to the inspiration and truth of your own nature.

Many people have found a particular connection with the picture of the statue of Padmasambhava called "Looks Like Me," which was made from life and blessed by him in the eighth century in Tibet. (See frontispiece.) Padmasambhava, by the enormous power of his spiritual personality, brought the teaching of Buddha to Tibet. He is known as the "second Buddha," and affectionately called "Guru Rinpoche," meaning "Precious Master," by the Tibetan people. Dilgo Khyentse Rinpoche said: "There have been many incredible and incomparable masters from the noble land of India and Tibet, the Land of Snows, yet of them all, the one who has the greatest compassion and blessing toward beings in this difficult age is Padmasambhava, who embodies the compassion and wisdom of all the buddhas. One of his qualities is that he has the power to give his blessing instantly to whoever prays to him, and whatever we may pray for, he has the power to grant our wish immediately."

Inspired by this, fix a copy of this picture at your eye level, and lightly set your attention on his face, especially on the gaze of his eyes. There is a deep stillness in the immediacy of that gaze, which almost bursts out of the photograph to carry you into a state of awareness without clinging, the state of meditation. Then leave your mind quietly, at peace, with Padmasambhava.

3. RECITING A MANTRA

A third technique, used a great deal in Tibetan Buddhism (and also in Sufism, Orthodox Christianity, and Hinduism), is uniting the mind with the sound of a *mantra.* The definition of mantra is "that which protects the mind." That which protects the mind from negativity, or that which protects you from your own mind, is called mantra.

When you are nervous, disoriented, or emotionally fragile, chanting or reciting a mantra can change the state of your mind completely, by transforming its energy and atmosphere. How is this possible? Mantra is the essence of sound, and the embodiment of the truth in the form of sound. Each syllable is impregnated with spiritual power, condenses a spiritual truth, and vibrates with the blessing of the speech of the buddhas. It is also said that the mind rides on the subtle energy of the breath, the prana, which moves through and purifies the subtle channels of the body. So when you chant a mantra, you are charging your breath and energy with the energy of the mantra, and so working directly on your mind and subtle body.

The mantra I recommend to my students is OM AH HUM VAJRA GURU PADMA SIDDHI HUM (Tibetans say: Om Ah Hung Benza

Guru Péma Siddhi Hung), which is the mantra of Padmasambhava, the mantra of all the buddhas, masters, and realized beings, and so uniquely powerful for peace, for healing, for transformation and for protection in this violent, chaotic age. Recite the mantra quietly, with deep attention, and let your breath, the mantra, and your awareness become slowly one. Or chant it in an inspiring way, and rest in the profound silence that sometimes follows.

Even after a lifetime of being familiar with the practice, I am still sometimes astonished by the power of mantra. A few years ago, I was conducting a workshop for three hundred people in Lyons, France, mostly housewives and therapists. I had been teaching all day, but they seemed really to want to make the most of their time with me and kept on asking me questions, relentlessly, one after another. By the end of the afternoon I was completely drained, and a dull and heavy atmosphere had descended over the whole room. So I chanted a mantra, this mantra I have taught you here. I was amazed by the effect: In a few moments I felt all my energy was restored, the atmosphere around us was transformed, and the whole audience seemed once again bright and enchanting. I have had experiences like these time and time again, so I know it is not just an occasional "miracle"!

What, then, should we "do" with the mind in meditation? Nothing at all. Just leave it, simply, as it is. One master described meditation as "mind, suspended in space, nowhere."

There is a famous saying: "If the mind is not contrived, it is spontaneously blissful, just as water, when not agitated, is by nature transparent and clear." I often compare the mind in meditation to a jar of muddy water: The more we leave the water without interfering or stirring it, the more the particles of dirt will sink to the bottom, letting the natural clarity of the water shine through. The very nature of the mind is such that if you only leave it in its unaltered and natural state, it will find its true nature, which is bliss and clarity.

So take care not to impose anything on the mind, or to tax it. When you meditate there should be no effort to control, and no attempt to be peaceful. Don't be overly solemn or feel that you are taking part in some special ritual; let go even of the idea that you are meditating. Let your body remain as it is, and your breath as you find it. Think of yourself as the sky, holding the whole universe.

A Delicate Balance

In meditation, as in all arts, there has to be a delicate balance between relaxation and alertness. Once a monk called Shrona was studying meditation with one of the Buddha's closest disciples. He had difficulty finding the right frame of mind. He tried very hard to concentrate, and gave himself a headache. Then he relaxed his mind, but so much that he fell asleep. Finally he appealed to Buddha for help. Knowing that Shrona had been a famous musician before he became a monk, Buddha asked him: "Weren't you a *vina* player when you were a layperson?"

Shrona nodded.

"How did you get the best sound out of your vina? Was it when the strings were very tight or when they were very loose?"

"Neither. When they had just the right tension, neither too taut nor too slack."

"Well, it's exactly the same with your mind."

One of the greatest of Tibet's many woman masters, Ma Chik Lap Drön, said: "Alert, alert; yet relax, relax. This is a crucial point for the View in meditation." Alert your alertness, but at the same time be relaxed, so relaxed in fact that you don't even hold onto an idea of relaxation.

Thoughts and Emotions: The Waves and the Ocean

When people begin to meditate, they often say that their thoughts are running riot, and have become wilder than ever before. But I reassure them and say that this is a good sign. Far from meaning that your thoughts have become wilder, it shows that *you* have become quieter, and you are finally aware of just how noisy your thoughts have always been. Don't be disheartened or give up. Whatever arises, just keep being present, keep returning to the breath, even in the midst of all the confusion.

In the ancient meditation instructions, it is said that at the beginning thoughts will arrive one on top of another, uninterrupted, like a steep mountain waterfall. Gradually, as you perfect meditation, thoughts become like the water in a deep, narrow gorge, then a great river slowly winding its way down to the sea, and finally the mind becomes like a still and placid ocean, ruffled by only the occasional ripple or wave.

Sometimes people think that when they meditate there should be no thoughts and emotions at all; and when thoughts and emotions do arise, they become annoyed and exasperated with themselves and think they have failed. Nothing could be further from the truth. There is a Tibetan saying: "It's a tall order to ask for meat without bones, and tea without leaves." So long as you have a mind, there will be thoughts and emotions.

Just as the ocean has waves, or the sun has rays, so the mind's own radiance is its thoughts and emotions. The ocean has waves, yet the ocean is not particularly disturbed by them. The waves are the *very nature* of the ocean. Waves will rise, but *where* do they go? Back into the ocean. And where do the waves come from? The ocean. In the same manner, thoughts and emotions are the radiance and expression of the *very nature* of the mind. They rise from the mind, but where do they dissolve? Back into the mind. Whatever rises, do not see it as a particular problem. If you do not impulsively react, if you are only patient, it will once again settle into its essential nature.

When you have this understanding, then rising thoughts only enhance your practice. But when you do not understand what they intrinsically are—the radiance of the nature of your mind—then your thoughts become the seed of confusion. So have a spacious, open, and compassionate attitude toward your thoughts and emotions, because in fact your thoughts are your family, the family of your mind. Before them, as Dudjom Rinpoche used to say: "Be like an old wise man, watching a child play."

We often wonder what to do about negativity or certain troubling emotions. In the spaciousness of meditation, you can view your thoughts and emotions with a totally unbiased attitude. When your attitude changes, then the whole atmosphere of your mind changes, even the very nature of your thoughts and emotions. When *you* become more agreeable, then *they* do; if you have no difficulty with them, they will have no difficulty with you either.

So whatever thoughts and emotions arise, allow them to rise and settle, like the waves in the ocean. Whatever you find yourself thinking, let that thought rise and settle, without any constraint. Don't grasp at it, feed it, or indulge it; don't cling to it and don't try to solidify it. Neither follow thoughts nor invite them; be like the ocean looking at its own waves, or the sky gazing down on the clouds that pass through it.

You will soon find that thoughts are like the wind; they come and go. The secret is not to "think" about thoughts, but to allow them to flow through the mind, while keeping your mind free of afterthoughts.

In the ordinary mind, we perceive the stream of thoughts as continuous; but in reality this is not the case. You will discover for yourself that there is a gap between each thought. When the past thought is past, and the future thought not yet arisen, you will always find a gap in which the Rigpa, the nature of mind, is revealed. So the work of meditation is to allow thoughts to slow down, to make that gap become more and more apparent.

My master had a student called Apa Pant, a distinguished Indian diplomat and author, who served as Indian ambassador in a number of capital cities around the world. He had even been the representative of the Government of India in Tibet in Lhasa, and for a time he was their representative in Sikkim. He was also a practitioner of meditation and yoga, and each time he saw my master, he would always ask him "how to meditate." He was following an Eastern tradition, where the student keeps asking the master one simple, basic question, over and over again.

Apa Pant told me this story. One day our master Jamyang Khyentse was watching a "Lama Dance" in front of the Palace Temple in Gangtok, the capital of Sikkim, and he was chuckling at the antics of the *atsara,* the clown who provides light relief between dances. Apa Pant kept pestering him, asking him again and again how to meditate, so this time when my master replied, it was in such a way as to let him know that he was telling him once and for all: "Look, it's like this: When the past thought has ceased, and the future thought has not yet risen, isn't there a gap?"

"Yes," said Apa Pant.

"Well, prolong it: *That* is meditation."

Experiences

As you continue to practice, you may have all kinds of experiences, both good and bad. Just as a room with many doors and windows allows the air to enter from many directions, in the same way, when your mind becomes open, it is natural that all kinds of experiences can come into it. You might experience states of bliss, clarity, or absence of thoughts. In one way these are very good experiences, and signs of progress in meditation. For when you experience bliss, it's a sign that desire has temporarily dissolved. When you experience real clarity, it's a sign that aggression has temporarily ceased. When you experience a state of absence of thought, it's a sign that your ignorance has temporarily died. By themselves they are good experiences, but if you get attached to them they become obstacles. Experiences are not realization in themselves; but if we remain free of attachment to them, they become what they really are, that is, materials for realization.

Negative experiences are often the most misleading because we usually take them as a bad sign. But in fact the negative experiences in our practice are blessings in disguise. Try not to react to them with aversion as you might normally do, but recognize them instead for what they truly are, merely experiences, illusory and dream-like. The realization of the true nature of the experience liberates you from the harm or danger of the experience itself, and as a result even a negative experience can become a source of great blessing and accomplishment. There are innumerable stories of how masters worked like this with negative experiences and transformed them into catalysts for realization.

Traditionally it's said that for a real practitioner, it's not the negative experiences but the good ones that bring obstacles. When things are going well, you have got to be especially careful and mindful so that you don't become complacent or over-confident. I remember what Dudjom Rinpoche once said to me when I was in the middle of a very powerful experience: "Don't get too excited. In the end, it's neither good nor bad." He knew I was becoming attached to the experience: *that* attachment, like any other, has to be cut through. What we have to learn, in both meditation and in life, is to be free of attachment to the good experiences, and free of aversion to the negative ones.

Dudjom Rinpoche warns us of another pitfall: "On the other hand, in meditation practice, you might experience a muddy, semiconscious, drifting state, like having a hood over your head: a dreamy dullness. This is really nothing more than a kind of blurred and mindless stagnation. How do you get out of this state? Alert yourself, straighten your back, breathe the stale air out of your lungs, and direct your awareness into clear space to freshen your mind. If you remain in this stagnant state, you will not evolve; so whenever this setback arises, clear it again and again. It is important to be as watchful as possible, and to stay as vigilant as you can."

Whatever method you use, drop it, or simply let it dissolve on its own, when you find you have arrived naturally at a state of alert, expansive, and vibrant peace. Then continue to remain there quietly, undistracted, without necessarily using any particular method. The method has already achieved its purpose. However, if you do stray or become distracted, then return to whatever technique is most appropriate to call you back.

The real glory of meditation lies not in any method but in its continual living experience of presence, in its bliss, clarity, peace, and most important of all, complete absence of grasping. The diminishing of grasping in yourself is a sign that you are becoming freer of yourself. And the more you experience this freedom, the clearer the sign that the ego and the hopes and fears that keep it alive are dissolving, and the closer you will come to the infinitely generous "wisdom of egolessness." When you live in that wisdom home, you'll no longer find a barrier between "I" and "you," "this" and "that," "inside" and "outside"; you'll have come, finally, to your true home, the state of non-duality.[8]

Taking Breaks

Often people ask: "How long should I meditate? And when? Should I practice twenty minutes in the morning and in the evening, or is it better to do several short practices during the day?" Yes, it is good to meditate for twenty minutes, though that is not to say that twenty minutes is the limit. I have not found that it says twenty minutes anywhere in the scriptures; I think it is a notion that has been contrived in the West, and I call it "Meditation Western Standard Time." The point is not how long you meditate; the point is whether the practice actually brings you to a certain state of mindfulness and presence, where you are a little open and able to connect with your heart essence. And five minutes of wakeful sitting practice is of far greater value than twenty minutes of dozing!

Dudjom Rinpoche used to say that a beginner should practice in short sessions. Practice for four or five minutes, and then take a short break of just one minute. During the break let go of the method, but do not let go of your mindfulness altogether. Sometimes when you have been struggling to practice, curiously, the very moment when you take a break from the method—if you are still mindful and present—is the moment when meditation actually happens. That is why the break is just as important a part of meditation as the sitting itself. Sometimes I say to students who are having problems with their practice to practice during the break and take a break during their meditation!

Sit for a short time; then take a break, a very short break of about thirty seconds or a minute. But be mindful of whatever you do, and do not lose your presence and its natural ease. Then alert yourself and sit again. If you do many short sessions like this, your breaks will often make your meditation more real and more inspiring; they will take the clumsy, irksome, rigidity and solemnity and unnaturalness out of your practice, and bring you more and more focus and ease. Gradually, through this interplay of breaks and sitting, the barrier between meditation and everyday life will crumble, the contrast between them will dissolve, and you will find yourself increasingly in your natural pure presence, without distraction. Then, as Dudjom

Rinpoche used to say, "Even though the meditator may leave the meditation, the meditation will not leave the meditator."

Integration: Meditation in Action

I have found that modern spiritual practitioners lack the knowledge of how to integrate their meditation practice with everyday life. I cannot say it strongly enough: to integrate meditation in action is the whole ground and point and purpose of meditation. The violence and stress, the challenges and distractions of modern life make this integration even more urgently necessary.

People complain to me, "I have meditated for twelve years, but somehow I haven't changed. I am still the same. Why?" Because there is an abyss between their spiritual practice and their everyday life. They seem to exist in two separate worlds, and not to inspire each other at all. I am reminded of a teacher I knew when I was at school in Tibet. He was brilliant at expounding the rules of Tibetan grammar, but he could hardly write one correct sentence!

How, then, do we achieve this integration, this permeation of everyday life with the calm humor and spacious detachment of meditation? There is no substitute for regular practice, for only through real practice will we begin to taste unbrokenly the calm of our nature of mind and so be able to sustain the experience of it in our everyday life.

I always tell my students not to come out of meditation too quickly: Allow a period of some minutes for the peace of the practice of meditation to infiltrate your life. As my master, Dudjom Rinpoche, said: "Don't jump up and rush off, but mingle your mindfulness with everyday life. Be like a man who's fractured his skull, always careful in case someone will touch him."

Then, after meditation, it's important not to give in to the tendency we have to solidify the way we perceive things. When you do reenter everyday life, let the wisdom, insight, compassion, humor, fluidity, spaciousness, and detachment that meditation brought you pervade your day-to-day experience. Meditation awakens in you the realization of how the nature of everything is illusory and dream-like; maintain that awareness even in the thick of samsara. One great master has said: "After meditation practice, one should become a child of illusion."

Dudjom Rinpoche advised: "In a sense everything is dream-like and illusory, but even so, humorously you go on doing things. For example, if you are walking, without unnecessary solemnity or self-consciousness, lightheartedly walk toward the open space of truth.

When you sit, be the stronghold of truth. As you eat, feed your negativities and illusions into the belly of emptiness, dissolving them into all-pervading space. And when you go to the toilet, consider all your obscurations and blockages are being cleansed and washed away."

So what really matters is not just the practice of sitting but far more the state of mind you find yourself in after meditation. It is this calm and centered state of mind you should prolong through everything you do. I like the Zen story in which the disciple asked his master:

"Master, how do you put enlightenment into action? How do you practice it in everyday life?"

"By eating and by sleeping," replied the master.

"But Master, everybody sleeps and everybody eats."

"But not everybody eats when they eat, and not everybody sleeps when they sleep."

From this comes the famous Zen saying, "When I eat, I eat; when I sleep, I sleep."

To eat when you eat and sleep when you sleep means to be completely present in all your actions, with none of the distractions of ego to stop you being there. This is integration. And if you really wish to achieve this, what you need to do is not just practice as an occasional medicine or therapy, but as if it were your daily sustenance or food. That is why one excellent way to develop this power of integration is to practice it in a retreat environment, far from the stresses of modern city life.

All too often people come to meditation in the hope of extraordinary results, like visions, lights, or some supernatural miracle. When no such thing occurs, they feel extremely disappointed. But the real miracle of meditation is more ordinary and much more useful. It is a subtle transformation, and this transformation happens not only in your mind and your emotions, but also actually in your body. It is very healing. Scientists and doctors have discovered that when you are in a good humor, then even the cells in your body are more joyful; and when your mind is in a more negative state, then your cells can become malignant. The whole state of your health has a lot to do with your state of mind and your way of being.

Inspiration

I have said that meditation is the road to enlightenment and the greatest endeavor of this life. Whenever I talk about meditation to my students, I always stress the necessity to practice it with resolute discipline and one-pointed devotion; at the same time, I always tell them how important it is to do it in as inspired and as richly creative a way as possible. In one sense meditation is an art, and you should bring to it an artist's delight and fertility of invention.

Become as resourceful in inspiring yourself to enter your own peace as you are at being neurotic and competitive in the world. There are so many ways of making the approach to meditation as joyful as possible. You can find the music that most exalts you and use it to open your heart and mind. You can collect pieces of poetry, or quotations or lines of teachings that over the years have moved you, and keep them always at hand to elevate your spirit. I have always loved Tibetan *thangka* paintings, and derive strength from their beauty. You too can find reproductions of paintings that arouse a sense of sacredness, and hang them on the walls of your room. Listen to a cassette tape of a teaching by a great master, or a sacred chant. You can make of the place where you meditate a simple paradise, with one flower, one stick of incense, one candle, one photograph of an enlightened master, or one statue of a deity or a buddha. You can transform the most ordinary of rooms into an intimate sacred space, into an environment where every day you come to the meeting with your true self with all the joy and happy ceremony of one old friend greeting another.

And if you find that meditation does not come easily in your city room, be inventive and go out into nature. Nature is always an unfailing fountain of inspiration. To calm your mind, go for a walk at dawn in the park, or watch the dew on a rose in a garden. Lie on the ground and gaze up into the sky, and let your mind expand into its spaciousness. Let the sky outside awake a sky inside your mind. Stand by a stream and mingle your mind with its rushing; become one with its ceaseless sound. Sit by a waterfall and let its healing laughter purify your spirit. Walk on a beach and take the sea wind full and sweet against your face. Celebrate and use the beauty of moonlight to poise your mind. Sit by a lake or in a garden and, breathing quietly, let your mind fall silent as the moon comes up majestically and slowly in the cloudless night.

Everything can be used as an invitation to meditation. A smile, a face in the subway, the sight of a small flower growing in the crack of a cement pavement, a fall of rich cloth in a shop window, the way the sun lights up flower pots on a window sill. Be alert for any sign of beauty or grace. Offer up every joy, be awake at all moments, to "the news that is always arriving out of silence."[9]

Slowly you will become a master of your own bliss, a chemist of your own joy, with all sorts of remedies always at hand to elevate, cheer, illuminate, and inspire your every breath and movement. What is a great spiritual practitioner? A person who lives always in the presence of his or her own true self, someone who has found and who uses continually the springs and sources of profound inspiration. As the modern English writer Lewis Thompson wrote: "Christ, supreme poet, lived truth so passionately that every gesture of his, at once pure Act and perfect Symbol, embodies the transcendent."[10]

To embody the transcendent is why we are here.

Notes

1. Thich Nhat Hanh, *Old Path, White Clouds* (Berkeley, CA: Parallax Press, 1991), 121.

2. Samsara is the uncontrollable cycle of birth and death in which sentient beings, driven by unskillful actions and destructive emotions, repeatedly perpetuate their own suffering. Nirvana is a state beyond suffering, the realization of the ultimate truth, or Buddhahood.

3. The ferocious wild animals that were a threat in ancient times have today been replaced by other dangers: our wild and uncontrolled emotions.

4. Marion L. Matics, *Entering the Path of Enlightenment: The Bodhicaryavatara of the Buddhist Poet Shantideva* (London: George, Allen and Unwin, 1971), 162.

5. Calm Abiding and Clear Seeing are the two central practices of Buddhist meditation, called in sanskrit *Shamatha* and *Vipashyana,* and in Tibetan *Shyiné* and *Lhaktong.* Their deepening and development forms the link between basic meditation practice and the more advanced meditation practices of Mahamudra and Dzogchen.

6. The future Buddha, Maitreya, is in fact portrayed sitting on a chair.

7. You may not be following this practice now, but keeping the eyes open creates an auspicious condition for your practicing in the future.

8. Although I have given here a full instruction on the practice, it should be borne in mind that meditation cannot truly be learned from a book, but only with the guidance of a qualified teacher.

9. Rainer Maria Rilke in *Duino Elegies.*

10. Lewis Thompson, *Mirror to the Light* (Coventure).

For information about Sogyal Rinpoche, his work and teaching program, his audio cassette tapes, and information on meditation courses and study groups, please contact: Rigpa National Office, P.O. Box 607, Santa Cruz, CA 95061–0607, telephone (408) 454–9103.

Contact the above address for Washington D.C., Boston, New York, Chicago, Seattle, Portland, San Francisco, Berkeley, San Diego, Ontario, Canada, and other cities. There are also Rigpa centers in Britain, France, Germany, Ireland, Australia, Netherlands, and Switzerland.